C000077179

Claire Salisbury is a Gestalt therapist, with a private practice in Northwest London. She has been involved with the National Stepfamily Association for over 2 years as a counsellor on their Helpline, has written various articles on family issues and has co-run therapy groups for parents.

Cheryl Walters is an individual, psychosexual and marital therapist in private practice, is Counselling Coordinator of the National Stepfamily Association, training the counsellors in stepfamily issues and has worked as an Honorary Psychotherapist at St. Mary's Hospital Paddington. She was a volunteer counsellor on the Helpline from 1988 - 1991.

The National Stepfamily Association
STEPFAMILY Publications

First published in 1997
by STEPFAMILY Publications

The National Stepfamily Association
Chapel House 18 Hatton Place
London EC1N 8RU

Registered Charity No 1005351
Company Limited by Guarantee No 2552166

Telephone: 0171 209 2460 (office)
0990 168 388 (Counselling line)

ISBN 1 873309 23 6

Printed by Lonsdale Press

CONTENTS

ACKNOWLEDGMENTS

We wish to thank our families and friends for their unstinting support and helpful feedback. Unaware, they have been a rich resource of knowledge which has facilitated the writing of this book.

Others who have contributed greatly to our thinking, knowledge and perceptions are our therapists, teachers, supervisors, other authors and colleagues. In particular we would like to mention Erica De'Ath who supportively encouraged this book to happen, the National Council of Voluntary Child Care Organisations for funding this project, the National Stepfamily Association Helpline which provided us with the issues that most concern stepfamilies, Simon Jackson for his inspiring and eloquent illustrations, Cartoonists: Tony Eagle, Louis Hellman, Steve Way, Ham, Larry, BRG and Sally Artz. Reviewers for their greatly appreciated constructive criticism: Hazel Allen, Dorit Braun, Pam Coney, Peter Coney and Deidre Sanders. In addition: Jacqui Brill, Aine Chambers and family, Jenny Cross and family, Danielle Gerrard and Ann Griffiths-Jones.

Finally our thanks to a richly inclusive book called 'A Celebration of Customs and Rituals of the World' which opened our eyes to the very many diverse occasions which propel families and friends to 'get together'.

FOREWORD

Deidre Saunders

As problem-page editor of The Sun and agony aunt at GMTV I hear every day from stepfamilies with problems. But this doesn't at all mean that I see stepfamilies as 'problem families', which is a label I know many rightly resent.

Finding yourself in some way a member of a stepfamily is now so common that it needs to be seen as a stage in life most of us will have to cope with sooner or later. Even if it's at one remove, such as being the brother or sister or parent of someone who's becoming a stepparent, how we react may well have a profound affect on that family's happiness and the children involved.

And just like other major transitions in life, it does bring stresses and conflicting emotions to the surface. When you think of the millions of words of advice poured out over decades to help us through other common life stages, such as arranging a wedding or having a baby, you realise how common it is to feel the need for guidance and how little there still is around for stepfamilies.

Even stepfamilies who have managed to navigate and negotiate their way around many of the stumbling blocks to creating a harmonious new family life can find themselves thrown into disarray by discovering their members are nursing all sorts of different assumptions and expectations about special get togethers, such as summer holidays, Christmas and birthdays.

My postbag tends to bulge as stepfamilies try to make seasonal arrangements, and I'm very glad that I will now be able to recommend this sympathetic and extremely practical guide to help them get happily all together.

SKILLS NEEDED FOR A
SUCCESSFUL STEPFAMILY!

How to care for, love, encourage and support yourself, your partner and the children whilst providing clear guidelines for behaviour, managing a household on a limited income and balancing your needs as a couple with the needs of the children and the extended family!

INTRODUCTION

Our original idea for this book was to write about holidays and stepfamilies. We soon realised that the issues we were grappling with could apply to all times that stepfamily members gather together. Recognising that it would be impossible to include every instance as this is such a broad subject, we have set examples to particular situations or events and urge you to think about them in the light of your own experiences. Although not all eventualities are covered, the issues that do arise are relevant to many different everyday stepfamily situations.

We want to entertain as well as inform the reader, to consider the serious and difficult aspects of stepfamily life, as well as the funny side. The book aims to be useful for children, young people and adults. In these pages you will find support and encouragement to find your own solutions, something to make you laugh and some helpful ideas.

There are many times when stepfamilies 'gather together'. There are the everyday situations such as mealtimes and weekends when different members of the family may be together. There are holidays; school holidays when children spend more time at home or stay away, family holidays in this country or abroad and the holiday periods at winter, spring and summer. Stepfamilies also gather at special events and celebrations such as birthdays, weddings, christenings, graduations, barmitzvahs, funerals and religious or spiritual festivals such as Diwali, Ramadan and Christmas.

Relationships in a family are complex. This is especially true in a stepfamily where children may belong to more than one family, where there may be difficult relationships with ex-partners and relatives and where both children and adults may have split loyalties. As stepfamilies develop, the members are negotiating their positions and security. These complexities mean that it becomes important to think through the implications of decisions and choices, whenever possible.

Life is a series of changing situations rather than fixed events and this is true of a stepfamily as well. It can be helpful to remember that while divorce may end quickly, the coming together and establishment of a stepfamily happens over a period of time – usually 2 to 10 years! Stepfamilies are hard work but they can also be a rewarding place to grow up in for adults and children alike.

For people going into a stepfamily situation, the new relationship doesn't start with a totally clean sheet. Stepfamilies often have a network of people who all need to be considered who may be male or female, full time or weekend parents, a new partner, a child or stepchild. You will *naturally* have strong emotions about everyone involved in your stepfamily. Also everybody concerned is going to have their own set of responses which may be different or similar to yours. This does not make things easy.

YES, SHE DOES HAVE MY HUSBAND'S NOSE. BUT HER EYES ARE MORE LIKE HER FATHER'S ......

None of this is anybody's fault and no one is to blame for how they are feeling. For example your child may have characteristics that remind you of your ex-partner and you may have mixed feelings about this. Your child may find it comforting to know that he is like his dad, while a new partner may find the similarity irritating and painful, seeing the child as a living reminder of the previous relationship.

There is no right way of parenting – there are as many different ways as there are families, and many are successful. No one is born knowing how to be a parent or stepparent, you learn from your own parents and 'on the job' and this is fine. It is helpful for stepparents to be able to acknowledge this and feel free at times to say to their children and stepchildren that they haven't the foggiest idea how to deal with a situation. To be able to do this will give the positive message to children that it is OK not to have all the answers.

It is important to remember that a new partner is not a new parent. Stepparents need to build a relationship with their stepchildren. One way of helping this process is for birth parents initially, to take responsibility for disciplining their own children so that the stepparent can have time to build up a friendship with their stepchildren. In this situation both adults need to discuss and agree such things as house rules and boundaries (where lines are drawn), with these being presented and enforced by the birth parent with the support and back up of their partner.

It is a misconception to blame all problems on being a stepfamily. All families are imperfect, however difficulties can be magnified in a stepfamily and children in stepfamilies often exhibit rejecting and problematic behaviour.

' DARLING, I WANT YOU TO MEET YOUR NEW MUMMY.
I'M SURE YOU'LL GET ON LIKE A HOUSE ON FIRE!'

Often adults forget to look at things from the point of view of the child. A lot of difficulties become clearer and easier to manage when the feelings behind behaviours are understood. The central point for a child in a stepfamily is that some form of loss is always involved. If a child feels abandoned he or she may find it safer to be angry or upset with a stepparent than to risk losing their birth parent even more than they already have. A child who is behaving badly may be missing the parent who has left and may be testing both parent and stepparent, to see if he or she is loved enough for them to stay whatever behaviour they exhibit.

Children are not consulted about whether their parents stay together, so have no reason to try and co-operate in any new arrangements, or even try to understand them. They can often only look at things from their own perspective, and see themselves as the losers. As children have no control over their parents' splitting-up, the only power they have lies in showing you their dissatisfaction. Children also tend to blame themselves when their parents separate, feeling that if they had behaved differently their parents might still be together.

All of us fall back on childish patterns when we are under stress, and may need to cling to the conviction that we are right – in order to feel 'safe'. A child or an adult can easily be seen as deliberately misbehaving, rather than that they are reacting to feeling unsafe and fearful. Putting yourself in the other person's shoes at such times can help to stop scapegoating and blaming. Remembering how you felt at a particular age/stage can also create a space for understanding or making allowances, and can permit you to negotiate compromises when tackling difficulties. It is natural for all stepfamily members at times to have ambivalent feelings (being in a state of feeling two conflicting emotions at the same time) - admitting ambivalent feelings, allows you to move towards looking for solutions.

Remember what is good for the parents may not necessarily be so for the children, and vice versa. This is why it is important to check out that your expectations are realistic and not assume that everyone feels as you do. Listen to children – don't steamroller them, but think of your own feelings too. The main difference between the parent and the stepparent is the parental love which can sustain the birth parents' relationship with their child almost no matter what. However, no parent likes their children all the time. There is no need to demand more of yourself as a stepparent than as a parent.

Another important point is that children are sensitive and are often quick to turn adult comments into a negative about themselves. For example, saying you have never loved a former partner may imply that you do not love or want a part of the child either. If you paint a picture of the absent parent as 'bad' and living with or marrying them as a 'mistake', then a child may interpret this as part of them being bad and a mistake. Sometimes we forget that a person can have failings as a partner and still be a good parent.

It can be a mistake to think that a clean break or lack of contact with the absent parent does not harm or mark a child in any way. Clearly defined regular access and continuity with absent parents is reassuring for small children, with arrangements being re-assessed with them as they grow, to incorporate their needs and social lives too.

Days that you think should be happy e.g. birthdays etc. may be extremely painful if the child is wanting to be with both birth parents and can't. Thinking and talking about events and how different situations will be managed beforehand is the first step towards understanding, negotiating and finding the unique way forward for your particular family.

Remember, divorce doesn't necessarily mean failure. Living in any family is hard work – daily and particularly at special times.

Chapter 1

DIVERSITY IN THE STEPFAMILY:
HABITS, ATTITUDES, VALUES AND RITUALS

Occasions when we get together can be a source of intense anxiety and people are often driven by an unconscious force to make others become like them, in order to reduce their own anxiety and feel safe.

We all come into a stepfamily with our own package of habits, attitudes, values and rituals. We started to put this package together in childhood as the result of experiences in our families of origin, at school, with friends and generally as years go by. The contents of this package provide a pattern for the way we live our lives. When a stepfamily is formed the lack of familiarity with others' ways can feel as if our pattern is threatened, causing us to be irritable and impatient amongst other things. This is why we try so hard to make everyone the same. These feelings occur in most families, but cause potentially greater problems in a stepfamily because of the added number of people involved at the 'beginning', each coming in with their own different pattern.

Habits, which are natural to each person and familiar to those who have always lived together, may become a source of irritation in new and developing relationships. They can serve to remind us how different we all are and it can be this show of difference that creates enormous stress and turns a stepfamily upside down.

We all tend to be unaware of the habits we have, and when told feel confronted and may deny or rationalise the habit. If you find yourself doing this, it can help to stop and think about it, and admit that there may be some truth in what you are being told.

It is a positive step when family members are able to tell each other constructively what bothers them, and be open to honest feedback so that each other's point of view can be understood. This does not mean that everyone has to immediately change, but honest communication makes it possible for differences to be accommodated and new ways of doing things to be explored. This is the way towards successful relationships. It takes a long time for a stepfamily to develop and function successfully and this needs to be viewed as an ongoing process

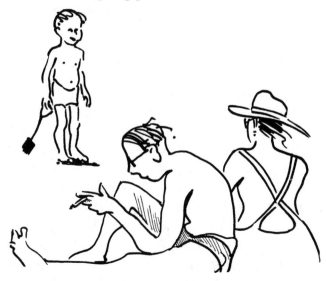

Sometimes people know that their habits are irritating to others and deliberately engage in them. This type of aggressive behaviour can send stepfamily life on a downhill slope, but it is important to consider what might be being expressed. If we are unable to accommodate, accept and live with other people's differences then we need to look at ourselves as well. The more irritated and impatient we are, the greater the problem is within us. The more stepfamily members are able to accept others, the more cohesive their family will become.

Our attitudes, like habits, come from many different life situations. Because stepfamilies are instant families, the people in them have had no time to get used to each other's attitudes. For example a parent may use consequences as a form of discipline, e.g. withdrawing treats if a child misbehaves, while their partner may believe that the only way to discipline is by getting the child's co-operation through talking together. One child's attitude is that homework is for goody-goodies and a stepsibling believes that it is actually fun to do. A new partner's attitude is that a variety of experiences make life interesting, the new stepfamily members think that people who always do different things are peculiar. Another way of looking at it is that learning to live with others who have different attitudes from ourselves can make life more interesting – we do not all have to be the same.

Values are the amount of importance we give to different things. Different people have different ideas about what is important and sometimes these clash. In a stepfamily it is inevitable that values about getting together times will be different. For example, one person might value mealtimes as a family but meet with opposition from other family members who place no value on this at all. A child might desperately want new clothes for a party only to find themselves with a stepparent who thinks this is unnecessary. A parent might value the occasional holiday without any of the children, only to find that a priority value of their new partner is to 'all be together on holidays'.

Values have varying degrees of strength and minor values may well be able to be accommodated and respected as an acceptable difference. It is when a stepfamily does not have major values in common, that they will find it difficult to resolve conflict in an honest and open way, or in extreme situations be able to stay together as a group. One way this might show itself is through irreconcilable differences in how to bring up children.

A way in which families develop an identity is to engage in family rituals. Rituals are the things you do, in the same way, at the same time, or in the same place, both at special and ordinary times. For example a birthday ritual might be to always turn off the light and bring a cake in with candles lit and sing happy birthday, or to always light the candles at the table, get them blown out and then sing happy birthday. Rituals are also part of the everyday pattern of events. For example you may have a set bedtime for your children, they brush their teeth, get themselves undressed, you read them a story and then kiss them goodnight; always in the same order. Variation from these rituals would be an exception. Special event rituals and day to day rituals serve to give order and familiarity to individual and family life.

Holidays are a time when different rituals held by stepfamily members (including extended family) might become highlighted. Different ideas about bedtime, how and when to open gifts, what meals to have, when and where to have an event, with whom to have it, and even which holidays to celebrate, can cause distress. For many adults and children, holidays are not holidays unless experienced in the same familiar way. For them it can be traumatic to break with traditions that have been part of their family life, which is why it is so hard to let go of them.

Despite these challenges, getting together can be a unique opportunity for stepfamilies to review their rituals, keep those they care about and let go or change those they have come to dislike. Through negotiation with all stepfamily members, rituals can be created that hold special meaning to all involved because they have been achieved through listening to and communicating with each other.

But remember genuine negotiation and compromise is not achieved without some loss to all parties. Creating your own rituals can serve to start a stepfamily bond in which it feels good to know that you are all getting something of what you want even when no one is getting all they want.

Round Table Meetings

Round table meetings are times when everybody gets together to talk about important family issues. These can be challenging, but they provide a forum in which each member has the opportunity to have their say, listen to others and learn to negotiate and compromise, which are all useful skills.

The following are suggestions for setting up such a meeting.

♦ Find a time that suits everyone.

♦ Hold the meeting in a neutral area where everyone is comfortable and has a space i.e.: around the kitchen table.

♦ Provide refreshments – the meeting might be hard work especially at the beginning. Treat yourself with crisps, nuts, fruit juice etc.

♦ Take the meeting seriously, provide pens, paper and a provisional agenda.
Make ground rules e.g.:
* No one walks out
* No one shouts
* Speak one at a time
* Respond one at a time
* Allow time for everyone
* No one hits anyone

♦ Agree how often to hold meetings.

♦ Make sure there is time in the meeting for any items that are not on the agenda.

It does take time for everyone to get used to the idea of family meetings and to establish your own style of meeting. If you persevere this can be a really valuable way of:

*   Getting to know each other
*   Spending time together
*   Sorting out difficult household issues i.e.: washing up
*   Arranging holidays and celebrations
*   Resolving conflict
*   Talking about difficult things

Good Luck!

What is it about creating family rituals that might be challenging for parents and stepparents, children and stepchildren?

♦ Talking about your differences and listening to other family members talk about theirs.

♦ Acknowledging that yours is not the only way to do things and that you may like or even prefer what another family member might suggest.

♦ Acknowledging that you too have habits, attitudes, values and rituals that might be strange or even difficult for others.

♦ Putting yourself in the other person's shoes and looking at the difficulty from their position.

♦ Beginning to value the uniqueness of the people around you and praising what is good even when it is different to your own pattern.

♦ Acknowledging that being a stepfamily presents challenges, changes and opportunities for growth.

At first these things may be difficult to do, but with practice you can get used to them and come to value the knowledge and understanding they offer you about yourself and others. You might be surprised at the light that is shed on your family's attitudes and behaviours, and your ability to understand them.

Chapter 2

STEPFAMILY GATHERINGS:
CELEBRATIONS, HOLIDAYS AND WEEKENDS

While adults and children may be aware of the need to change and move on, at times we all experience feelings of sadness and a longing that we could go back to how things were. This sense of loss is always more painful at family times of celebration such as weddings, birthdays and graduations, in fact anytime when families come together, including funerals.

For a child moving between two stepfamilies, they also have to remember which family does things which way. Adults need to allow children the flexibility to move in and out of the different families they belong to and support them to feel that difference is a positive thing. It is helpful when both adults and children are open to the idea that different ways of doing things can be fine; so that there is not the choice of this or that (exclusive) but this and also that (inclusive).

Arguments about how, when and where we celebrate festivals and events are usually not about the happening itself but how we feel about ourselves and the other people involved. The thing that is being fought over is not the event itself but what it means to each individual, adult and child. When disagreement in a new stepfamily occurs over some family members wanting to do something one way and others another, argument may be fueled by a feeling that a link with the past is at stake, or by the need to feel welcomed or central to the family.

At times you may well be tempted to throw up the whole thing in despair. If you try to work out what each person is asking for and what they may really be wanting and needing, then you are on the road to talk about ways some of these needs can be met, which will make you feel more content. You can begin to find out how you can celebrate in a way that offers something for all of you.

Expect less of yourself and forgive more. You may not be realising to what degree any problems that arise can be attributed to your emotions and interpretations of what is going on, rather than the situation itself. As an adult you bear the responsibility for what happens in your new family; recognise and explore your own feelings and those of the other people involved. Allow yourself to recognise how and why your feelings and the children's feelings may differ as this may help you all be more tolerant of each other.

Celebration days can be extremely painful if a child wants to be with both their birth parents and this is not possible, if children and stepchildren are being given unequal presents, or for many other reasons. People often behave unfairly without being aware of it, because they themselves have been subjected to unfair treatment and see this as normal. This can be highlighted at celebration times when everyone wants things to be perfect.

We all need to be rewarded, to be praised, thanked and appreciated, but sometimes we forget how much we need to value others and to be valued by them.

Often we forget how easy it is to give pleasure and how a little would mean a lot e.g.: a kind word, a hug, giving a comic or a bunch of flowers.

Possible Problems	Potential Solutions
Encompassing changes in routine. Both children and adults are likely to bring customs from another family and may feel unhappy if asked to unwrap presents or eat a special occasion meal at a different time from usual.	Talk together with children about changes in their and your usual customs. Listen to adults and children's responses and suggest ways in which you might meet some of everyone's needs.
Making amicable arrangements for children to see all parents and relatives over holiday periods. Deciding who should visit and when can cause anxieties and disagreements for both adults and children, especially if a parental split remains acrimonious.	Plan well ahead. As far as possible talk to ex-partners, making a note of and confirming decisions. If you agree times to pick up or drop off children, keep to your word. Children need to feel sure of their parents and a clear routine will help them feel more secure.
Pressure from several sets of grandparents to see children may cause the couple to feel unable to please everybody, leading to feelings of guilt and frustration that in turn get acted out in the couple relationship.	Stagger visits to grandparents and relatives rather than attempt the Herculean task of cramming visits into one or two days. e.g. extend Christmas to include New Year.
New partners may feel resentful of parenting responsibilities. Children as a consequence may feel unwanted and confused about where they stand with Mum or Dad's new partner.	Don't force a new partner to accept your children if they are not ready to do so. It might be better to introduce them at a less stressful time than a family occasion or event, so that you are free to give your attention.

Possible Problems	**Potential Solutions**
Competition may arise between children and adults for gifts and time spent together. The child who feels abandoned by an absent parent may take their anger and disappointment out on a stepparent or refuse to join in family games.	In order to overcome the difficulties of who does what at family gatherings call a 'round table meeting'. Ask each family member to offer suggestions to create the get together they would really enjoy so that everyone gets something of what they want.

All families have rules and assumptions, some of which are unspoken. As parents we make rules for our family such as when bedtime is, what times children are allowed out until etc. There are also rules that everybody understands but nobody ever speaks about. These often are stronger because they are unspoken and family members might never recognise them unless they were pointed out. An example of an unspoken rule might be 'you never talk about family business to someone outside' and no family member ever does. Families also have unspoken assumptions, which are things that we take to be true without proof. An example might be assuming that people do not argue in other families.

Not all rules and assumptions are realistic, we learn them from our childhood families, or pick up idealistic family images from television and advertising. Trying to apply unrealistic rules and assumptions to our families can make us unhappy during times together, feeling as if we can't do anything right.

As each family has a different set of rules and assumptions, this can be problematic in stepfamilies where some members belong to more than one household; for example when children spend weekdays with their mother and stepfather and weekends with their father and stepmother. The children then find themselves in a position where they have to adapt as they move between one household with one set of rules and assumptions to another household with an entirely different set. When a child moves in and out of households everybody else has to adjust as well, but this can be particularly difficult for children to manage.

Among the times when unrealistic rules and assumptions can make us unnecessarily miserable are when members of stepfamilies decide to go away together, maybe for a day trip, to a place of interest, a visit to relatives, a picnic or a holiday away from home, in this country or abroad. We can find ourselves feeling dissatisfied and pressurised if what happens does not happily match up with our expectations of what we think should happen.

We have listed some common assumptions and rules that people apply to holidays away (as well as other situations) and which don't work. Next to each one is a more realistic way of looking at the same situation, 'an antidote' which if taken to heart will ease pressure, and make it potentially more likely for stepfamily members to get along together.

Assumption	**Solution**
Everybody has to be happy all the time.	It's natural to be happy sometimes and not at others. If you try and be happy all the time you will collapse under the pressure.
We all have to be together all the time.	All of us need times when we are alone and have times when we would like company. An accepting attitude towards this will help you all relax.
We've all got to like each other.	It is impossible to guarantee that you will like each other and you don't have to. It is important to respect each other and not be abusive either emotionally or physically.
Adults have to love children all the same.	To expect this is unfair on you and impossible, however it is important to treat all children equally.
Children have to love all the adults all the same.	To expect this is unfair on them and impossible. If you treat children fairly and with respect they will learn to do the same.

Assumption	**Solution**
Everyone else is having a wonderful time.	We all tend to think this about each other when in fact everyone else is muddling through just like you.
Adults never make mistakes.	Actually we all do. It is helpful if we can acknowledge our mistakes and say we are sorry sometimes.
We must never change our minds.	This way of thinking can get us stuck and inflexible.

It is generally easier to think of problems than solutions, so we recommend setting aside time to think about the unspoken rules and assumptions in your family, consider possible solutions of your own, and stretch your mind to think about the positive aspects of your stepfamily.

Chapter 3

THE CHRISTMAS PERIOD
AND OTHER FESTIVALS
(see back page)

Whether Christian, Jewish, Muslim, Hindu or another religion or culture, you will have events and festivals designed to include all members of the family. Stepfamilies can find these times particularly stressful, expensive and difficult to arrange. As mentioned before, special events can bring their own complexities when family members who do not usually meet get together.

Here we have chosen to focus on the Christmas period. This time is difficult to ignore if you live in the United Kingdom, and the stepfamily issues that arise at this time are relevant to many other religious and cultural festivals.

Christmas time can be fun. Many of us - religious or otherwise - enjoy Christmas trees, decorations, and the spirit of generosity that surrounds Christmas. Shop windows display gifts, toys, trinkets and clothes. Streets and houses are decorated with tinsel and lights, food stores stock up with a glut of Christmas goods – turkeys, puddings and pies, crackers and sprouts. Carols are played on the radio and there is a general air of excitement on the streets. Most people, one way or another, find themselves caught up in the preparations for Christmas day.

However there is another side to the celebrations. Both adults and children tend to have high expectations of Christmas, thinking that it might make everything better, and therefore it can be a time of bitter disappointment. People who are on their own can feel extremely lonely and there is a high suicide rate at this time of year. Christmas is painful if the main effect of all the activity surrounding it reminds you of family members you are separated from, or conflicts in your current family.

As a stepfamily is often very extended – with more than one set of parents and relations, Christmas can become a feat of superhuman organisation as well as being extremely expensive. There are so many people and so many issues to consider.

" FINE – SO NEXT WEEKEND YOURS GO TO BRENDA, MINE GO TO NICK, UNA'S COME TO US, OURS GO TO MOTHER . . . "

* You may want time with your stepchildren and their birth father or mother does as well.
* You may have to spend the time with your stepchildren and not be with your birth children – when you would like to.
* Your children may want to be with you and their stepfamily as well.
* Children may want to spend Christmas Day with both parents.

These things can make everyone end up feeling very split.

There is no universal solution to these difficulties. You will find it easier to cope if you do not look for perfection and think about your own needs as well as those of others. If you find yourself running around after others, without making sure that you also get some of what you want, you are in danger of feeling drained and resentful by the end of the Christmas period.

Christmas is a time that can be very difficult for children when their parents live in different households. It is easy for them to feel split by their loyalties. They may want to spend time with both parents and be scared of hurting one of them. Be sensitive to this, and consider how you may accommodate their needs as well as your own.

Don't make the children choose between one parent and another, this can be damaging and is unfair on the child. Sort arrangements out between yourselves and allow yourself to be content, if not happy, with what is agreed.

Suggestions:

♦ Get together with your family and make a list of what each member of the family wants to happen around Christmas. In your list include the wishes of yourself, partner, children (if old enough), grandparents, ex-partners etc. Discuss the list together and incorporate as much as is realistically possible into your plans.

♦ Think about what is really important to you and if possible, prioritise it.

♦ Use a calendar to map everybody's availability.

♦ Put in time for yourself and your family to be on your own together.

♦ Make a list of who needs to see whom.

♦ Make a list of jobs that need doing and allocate them between you.

♦ Is it possible? If it does not look possible, see if you can find some creative solutions.

A Stepfamily Christmas Story

One stepfamily had two children who lived partly with their mother and partly with their father and stepmother. Both the parents wanted to spend time at Christmas with the children and because they were not getting on very well, and lived in different houses, this caused friction.

Eventually, the father and stepmother arranged to have Christmas with the children on Christmas Eve rather than on Christmas day. This was a particularly good solution for them because the father was Danish and in Denmark Christmas Eve is the most important day of Christmas. They were therefore able to have a traditional Danish Christmas with the children. The children spent Christmas day with their mother and had a traditional English meal with her.

The children found it a bit difficult having to leave one house on Christmas morning to go to the other, however they benefited from having the two Christmases, with two lots of presents and two different meals. The mother was able to go out on Christmas Eve, which was what she liked to do and the father and stepmother appreciated having a quiet Christmas day together.

Stepfamilies are often stretched financially, with parents supporting children in more than one household. At Christmas, the amount of family members can make present giving particularly expensive for both adults and children in a stepfamily. Children may have grandparents and stepgrandparents, two sets of parents, stepsiblings etc. Parents may have stepchildren as well as their birth children to consider. One way of tackling stretched finances could be to talk through money restrictions with the members of your household, discussing what you can and cannot afford. This will give everyone the opportunity to be involved, help to lower expectations and to make less extravagant gifts acceptable.

Giving presents to people in our families can be very enjoyable, it is also a way of expressing how you feel about each other. This is fine when the message is that you are fond of each other, however in a stepfamily there is likely to be a mixture of feelings, and some family members may not feel that they want to give to each other. This can particularly be an issue for stepgrandparents and stepgrandchildren who often do not feel much connection with each other, however it can also be true for stepparents and stepchildren.

The following are a list of issues that may arise around gift giving.

♦ **Rivalry**

In a stepfamily issues of rivalry and competition between siblings may be heightened. This can be most intense at times of gift giving. If for example you give your own child a bigger gift than you give your stepchild you could be seen to be making a clear statement of who is your favourite. Consider the implications of the size and expense of the gifts you are giving.

♦ **Split Loyalties**

Children may experience conflict when choosing presents.

For example, children living away from a parent often feel they want to compensate by buying a special present for them. If they have limited money this may mean having to choose between their stepparent and their birth parent, or having to buy a smaller present for their parent than they want to.

At times like Christmas the split loyalties that children feel become apparent. It will help them if you are able to understand this and talk to them about it.

♦ **Hurt**

As a stepparent, it may be hurtful to see a stepchild wanting to give a bigger present to their birth parent than you, if you are spending your time bringing them up. A birth parent may well feel the same in the reverse situation.

This is a situation where you will serve your family best by calling on all the understanding and tolerance you can muster. Unlike adults, children are unable to see things in perspective. If they want to show their parent they love them and you demand recognition as well, they may feel that you are trying to stop them from loving their parent and resent you for it.

Many stepchildren feel that they did not chose their stepparents and if possible would like to be able to live with both their birth parents. This is a natural feeling and it will help you if you can be patient and remember that it takes time for stepfamilies to become more unified.

◆ Competition between families

The size and value of presents can impact on other branches of the family. It is easy for stepparents and ex-partners to compete for the affection of children through gifts.

Many parents will compensate their feelings of guilt through buying special and expensive presents for their children, whether or not the family the children live with can afford to do the same.

When giving to your children, consider whether in doing so you are supporting their best interests or whether you are trying to make up for some lack in your relationship with them. Remember that presents do not make up for quality time and attention or for such necessities as food and clothing.

Chapter 4

FOOD AND EATING TOGETHER

The style in which food is provided differs from family to family. As we grow up, our parents provide nourishment by feeding us in a particular way. We learn styles of cooking, table manners and food behaviour from infancy and we use this information to help us feed our ourselves and our families when we grow up.

Food is a social currency. Not only do we eat because we need to, but also because it is enjoyable. Many people pride themselves on cooking as a form of giving – if someone likes their food, it means that they are nourishing them well and they get a glow of pleasure and feel accepted. The drawback of this is that if their food is rejected then they feel as if they are being rejected. Therefore this can become an area where approval and disapproval is expressed through like and dislike.

A new stepfamily consists of members from at least two previous families, with different expectations, likes and dislikes.

It is not surprising that mealtimes in such a family can be difficult, as it is around the table that many differences become apparent. For example, as a child it may be impossible not to compare the cooking of your stepmother with the cooking of your birth mother, who isn't there. You may feel that to like your stepparent's cooking would mean that you are rejecting your birth parent. As a stepparent you may think your stepchildren have bad table manners, or your table manners may be more relaxed than they are used to. You may be sitting round the table with people you don't like.

These considerations mean that while meals can be a pleasant time where families share food and each other's company they can just as easily be difficult, tense and argumentative.

Humans are territorial beings with a natural tendency to protect their own ways of doing things and to criticize and reject others. You may remember incidents when you have had to meet new people who matter such as prospective in-laws. In such a situation while wanting to be accepted and liked by these new people who are going to be part of your life, you are also looking and judging, wondering if you want to be involved and associated with them. This can cause extreme feelings of shyness, anxiety and criticism. When stepfamilies first start spending time together they are in a similar situation.

Mealtimes, when people display their manners and tastes, are times when acceptable behaviour is at the forefront. Members of new stepfamilies look at each other and wonder whether they like what they see, whether they can change what they don't like and whether they are themselves acceptable. This initial process is common to all stepfamilies. As people get to spend more time together the feelings can become less extreme as they begin to accept each other's differences, however this isn't always the case. Sometimes difficult situations get worse before they start to get better.

If your mealtimes are fraught with quarrels and bad feelings, it may help to remember that the process of acceptance usually takes several years. A lot of anxiety is caused by expectations that 'everything should be all right' in the early years of a stepfamily's life. The truth is that families who manage to stay together 'gel' and develop tastes, habits and patterns that belong to them.

You are most likely to succeed in staying together if you are able to be flexible enough to tolerate differences and have some understanding of the emotional pressures that affect the various members of your family.

The following is the story of the development of a family that became a stepfamily. It shows the changes that the family had to make when accommodating new members reflected in the style of foods they ate.

Stephanie married when she and her partner were vegetarian. She had two children who had never eaten meat. Stephanie's husband liked very plain wholefoods and although this was not entirely Stephanie's style, a lot of the food they ate was based on this, so they ate brown rice and bread, and very few dairy products. Her husband hated tomatoes and potatoes so they rarely ate these.

cont.

When their marriage broke down Stephanie lived on her own and chose food that was more of her own personal taste such as cheese, eggs and milk, fish on occasions and tomato pasta sauces. She then met John and they began to eat meat at restaurants, and to cook sausages for the children.

John spent more and more time with the family and Stephanie began to cook meat at home finding that she liked it. She still ate quite a lot of wholefoods, liked brown bread and discouraged eating sugar. The children weren't sure about meat and resented John, thinking that if it hadn't been for him they would still be vegetarian, and still living with their father.

John and Stephanie moved in together, and John's son Dave came to live with them. Dave liked chips, tomato ketchup and burgers and drank lots of cola. He did not like wholefoods at all. Stephanie found that she disapproved of Dave's eating habits and wanted to change them. She also felt that most of Dave's behaviour did not fit in with the family. Although she wanted to get on with him she found it was difficult and he irritated her. Dave didn't like a lot of the food that Stephanie cooked and often left it. They did not like each other much at that time.

As time went on, Dave and Stephanie got used to each other. After five years Stephanie's children got used to John and Dave, and the whole family argued less often. Their eating habits had changed as well. Dave ate a larger variety of foods than he did previously, and usually ate what Stephanie or John cooked for him. All the children ate meat, which was served at most meals, and the whole family ate lots of salad and occasionally chips.

At first everybody ate together but when the children were older they sometimes cooked for themselves so that they could go out while Stephanie and John ate later.

Stephanie and John developed a new style of eating for their family. It was unique to them and was based on a mixture of all the different styles and tastes brought in by the various family members. They also became flexible, as their family grew older so that the habit of when they ate changed. At the same time as the stepfamily was working out how to live together they created a new food style. This was all part of the process of becoming a cohesive stepfamily with its own way of doing things, where everybody felt they belonged.

Food is often a good way of melting a frosty atmosphere when people are feeling awkward with each other. A good meal can be welcoming and can break the ice. Events such as dinner parties are an example of this, when people relax over food. Also starting an occasion with a tea party can free children up who are finding it difficult to relax with each other, so that they are more able to play together.

One stepfamily had children that did not live with them all the time. They found that when the stepchildren came to stay with the family there was a difficult period before everybody was used to being with each other again. They invented the unbirthday party, which is a party just for its own sake, no special occasion needed. They held unbirthday parties when they first got together after a break. This was a successful solution for them, as everybody relaxed over the food and party atmosphere and it set them off on a good footing for their time together.

**There's no need to explain everyone,
just let them get on with it!**

This is an example of a stepfamily creating a new ritual for their situation. As it was successful, it became part of their family's culture and as such will probably be used by the different members when they form their own families in the future.

Chapter 5

SITTING TOGETHER

Whenever people get together for any length of time they sit. This might be around a table, on sofas and armchairs, on cushions or stools or in the front and backs of cars. Wherever (and however) people choose to sit expresses something about how they feel. For example, they may sit next to someone they feel comfortable with or whom they wish to unite with, sit in a position they think is special such as the head of the table, never quite know where to put themselves, or stand around awkwardly.

Members of a stepfamily may be in the process of negotiating their position with each other. How confident they are will depend on how long the family has been together and how successfully they have managed this area. In the first few years when the stepfamily is establishing itself, the different members will be working towards accepting and respecting each other, and towards becoming secure enough to have some stability. This can be difficult in a fairly new stepfamily where often not everyone is sure whether they like or want each other, let alone accept each other and feel comfortable about having a place.

A lot can be understood about the underlying feelings held by different family members through looking at the significance of where they place themselves when they get together either casually or formally. How people feel about their position in the family can be expressed through where they sit and seats are often given to or taken by different family members as a way of stating this.

It might be helpful in seeing how this works by picturing the following situations

♦ A family where stepfather always sits in the big arm chair while mother sits next to him, and the children sit on the sofa.

♦ A family member who never sits with the rest of the family.

♦ A child sitting at the head of the dinner table while everyone else sits along the sides.

♦ A stepfamily where the visiting children sit together on one side of the dinner table or on a chair nearest the door in the living room.

Having a seat - or a regular place means that you have an accepted place in the family and if your seat is in an important place it means you have an important position.

Because of this, seats can be used to express competition and conflict in a family.

Consider the following:

♦ A boy sits in his stepfather's chair whenever he can. *He may be feeling that if his stepfather were not there, then he would be the man in the family.*

♦ One of the children may rarely be able to find themselves a seat, and does not claim one. *She may feel that she has no place and does not have the confidence to insist on it.*

♦ A stepmother feels that she cannot ask a child who is sitting next to her father to leave her seat. *She may be waiting for the father to tell the child so that she feels that she has a place with him and is wanted.*

A common issue that illustrates the significance of seating is – who sits in the front of the car?

Most families and stepfamilies have arguments and disputes around who sits where in a car. The front seat is often perceived to have a high status, with adults or older children being given this place.

This is a situation taken from real life in the early days of a stepfamily.

The father, stepmother and son/stepson were on holiday and the stepmother sat in the front of the car for most of the journey. At one point the son asked his father if he could sit in the front and his father agreed.

In this situation the stepmother had a range of feelings.

She felt jealous and competitive of her stepson.

She thought her partner was putting his son before her and she did not like it

She felt bad because she thought that she should not have those sorts of feelings

She thought that she was being treated as if she was a child and worse than her stepson.

She would like to have liked her partner to ask about her feelings because then he would have been recognising that her feelings were important.

She realised that even if she had been asked, she would not have liked her stepson to sit in the front of the car because she felt that was her place.

Later on in their relationship the stepmother felt more confident and was able to say to her partner that her place was important. This allowed her feelings and thoughts to change.

She began to think that her stepson might be jealous of her being with his father.

She thought that perhaps her stepson had bad feelings about her – and that he also felt bad at times.

She thought her feelings were understandable and felt less bad about them.

She understood her stepson more, accepted and liked him better.

She still felt that she would like to be asked if she minded giving up her seat but having chosen not to give it up, felt fine about that.

This situation illustrates some of the feelings that surround seating issues. It also shows that relationships change in a stepfamily. As the stepmother became more secure, she was able to look at the situation without being threatened by it. This gave space for her to make a decision about a course of action that felt right to her, without being confused by her difficult feelings.

Every family needs to decide for themselves the way that feels best for them to deal with situations. It helps if you are able to discuss things with each other. Remember there is no right way, but there are ways that will suit you.

Seating issues are often about acceptance, status and having a place. It can be daunting to try and make a place for yourself in a new stepfamily, and there may be various pressures that make it feel like trying to swim upstream.

For an adult it can be difficult to establish your position if you are unsure of your right to do so. If you are new in a stepfamily, and it is your intention to stay there, then everyone will feel more secure if you claim your place clearly, even if you do not feel fully confident in doing so. In general, children feel safer when adults take charge and take their position, providing it is done in a matter of fact way and not in an aggressive manner.

However, children often do not like decisions adults have made that affect them. It is therefore important that adults listen to children and consider their point of view. Listening to children does not mean that you have to change your mind (although you may decide to).

It helps if all members of a stepfamily understand that new arrangements with people who they don't know very well can feel difficult, and uncomfortable. This is quite natural and as you get to know each other more, you will feel better about letting each other have a place.

It is important that you think about situations when they arise and consider carefully what might be going on 'behind the scenes', so that you can make your decisions with as much information as possible. Be creative and inventive in finding solutions to your difficulties. You may be surprised at how good this might leave you feeling.

Chapter 6

CAN'T YOU LEAVE EACH OTHER ALONE?

It is a fact, like it or not, that we are sexual beings. Sexuality is therefore around on most occasions, from visiting weekends to holidays away from home and all the various get together times in between. Sexual feelings are expressed in conscious and unconscious ways, some of which seem natural and comfortable and others that may not.

In new relationships sexual desires are usually a powerful force for getting together. In stepfamilies there are however often financial restrictions and difficulties with childcare, which may mean that children are around all the time, and can inhibit spontaneity. Time on your own as a couple is crucial to a healthy and fulfilling relationship.

One of the most common stepfamily couple complaints is 'we can never find time to be alone'.

When children and teenagers become aware that a parent has a sexual relationship with someone who is not their other parent, it can be a time of great emotional confusion. It may represent the end of the hope that their parents would get back together. Also it is easier to ignore parental sexuality which began before you were born and had become confined to the privacy of the parental bedroom, than adult sexuality which is growing in front of your eyes, like cuddling on the sofa, kissing in the hallway or exchanging seductive glances. Feelings of joy for the parent may be mixed with envy, guilt, anger, anxiety, hate and sadness as children try to make sense of what is happening and the impact it is having on them.

Teenagers are commonly heard to say 'I cannot imagine my parents doing it!'. Parents who do not show open affection, often seem sexless to their children. When a stepfamily couple shows appropriate love for each other, like holding hands, in front of their own and each other's children, they become role models for a loving partnership. As long as their behaviour does not involve explicit sexual behaviour, the children are receiving valuable lessons for their own lives as to how to 'be' in a relationship. It can sometimes be the first time this is experienced by the children, so it is natural for them to have mixed emotions like pleasure, embarrassment, or angry feelings. However a child living in this situation may feel more secure now that they are living with a loving couple. Adjusting to the sexual change takes time for all concerned. If a child seems unwilling to accept a parent's new sexual relationship they may be trying to protect themselves from their own anxiety and discomfort. Everyone may well be suffering the adjustment to the changes, but it often is the children and teenagers who become the easiest target for adult frustration or apathy if acceptance doesn't happen as quickly as the adults would like.

Couples need privacy and this means putting in place boundaries that were not necessary before. e.g. closing the bedroom door at night or not letting children into bed with you. In such situations the children may feel as if they are being excluded, and the truth is that they are. This can be hard for them and for you, however it is important for the couple to be able to have exclusive time to themselves.

If you make it a priority you can choose to make time for yourselves, however it stretches your ingenuity, be it half a day once a month or an hour each evening once the children are in bed. Discover what can work for both of you and make that protected time together. Remember that the key to stepfamily stability is the quality of the couple relationship.

This takes us back to the type of self-worth that allows a parent to negotiate protected time with a partner. Looking after your relationship by making time for yourself strengthens you as a couple and you will be better able to meet children's needs when they are not felt to be impinging upon or infringing your own needs. Respect, tolerance, co-operation, responsibility and compassion are likely to be features of families where self-esteem is high most of the time and where disappointments and failures are seen as temporary states and not experienced as a devastating and desperate personal defeat.

Finding a way to balance needs between family members, means having to be able to see situations and behaviours from the point of view of others, setting reasonable boundaries and having the courage to allow a dialogue from all parties around issues of sexuality and privacy.

Being able to see situations or behaviours from the point of view of a child (or indeed anyone else) comes naturally to an adult who has had enough good attention given to them in their own childhood. This enables us to feel secure and not personally threatened by the needs of others. However many of us do not feel secure in this way. This makes it more difficult, but not impossible, as it is a matter of developing new skills as we go along. Sometimes it is helpful to get support in the form of counselling, to enable us to look after ourselves and our families.

It is a good idea to allow time alone for each different permutation in the stepfamily adult/child structure so that individual relationships can grow. 10 minutes each week protected time can be all it needs to help individuals become less strange and more familiar with each other. Always listen, take seriously and consider any comment a child or adult makes.

Allow room for each person's different feelings - you do not all have to think or be the same to have a successful family - difference can be stimulating and broadening if you can give permission for it to co-exist alongside the similarities.

Try to imagine what it is about these particular situations that might be difficult for both parent/stepparent and child/stepchild?'

♦ Watching a parent hold hands with someone who is not your other parent.

♦ Feeling uninhibited enough to show affection to your partner in front of your and/or his children.

♦ Making love with a new partner for the first time in the family home.

♦ Talking with the children and asking them what they feel comfortable with and what troubles them.

♦ Accepting children's feedback and respecting their thoughts and feelings.

♦ Talking and listening to adults and accepting and respecting their thoughts and feelings.

You will see from doing this that it can be difficult for everybody to negotiate a new sexual adult relationship in a stepfamily. Having some idea of the things that you and other family members may find challenging will help you find ways of being sensitive to, and meeting your own and others' needs in this situation.

CONCLUSION

Having read this booklet you might well be feeling that a stepfamily is the last thing you want to become, too many difficulties and too much hard work! However, we hope that the positive and creative aspects of living in step have also captured your attention. We realise that while we have listed skills to aspire to, and various ways of understanding each other, these take time to develop and everyone will make mistakes along the way.

Common themes run through all stepfamily situations, which is why many areas in this book overlap. The overriding message is that the way to succeed with your stepfamily is to keep going, and not to be too discouraged when things become difficult. It really does take years for a stepfamily to become cohesive, and in the meantime there will be times when it seems as if you will never find a way to get together satisfactorily. However there are many successful stepfamilies who have been through extremely difficult situations, and have found that they now have good relationships with each other, apparently against all odds.

Stepfamilies have suffered from a bad press for far too long and we would like to redress the balance. With the increase in divorce and the breakdown of relationships, stepfamilies have become a valuable new form of extended family. When successful, stepfamily members of all ages gain the benefit of being connected to a wide range of related people. Stepfamilies are a positive investment in family life and are created because we all want successful relationships. They are a step towards healing, and learning from past experiences that sadly came to an end.

One of the major difficulties when the going gets tough, is knowing whether to hang in there or to cut your losses and get out. In first relationships there is usually time for courting before a family is built, we are more likely to know how we feel about our partner and are in a position to decide whether or not to have children. This is not the case in a stepfamily. We experience the first raptures but have no chance to consolidate these on the longer term before children arrive, as children may be already part of the equation. Furthermore the children are someone else's, which can make us feel rejecting of them, and we have to make a new relationship with them, which they have no choice about, and which may cause them to reject us. There is very little information about what to expect, so when things get tough we are not certain whether it is worth continuing, particularly in the light of past memories or experiences of failed relationships. How the relationship will work without children living at home is likely to remain an unknown until they have grown up and left!

We have emphasised the importance of adults making room for nurturing their relationship. Not only does it feel good, it also oils the wheels of family life and acts as a buffer against the hard times. You may well feel that at times you've sacrificed too much for your stepfamily, but you might well be losing even more if you totally give up and go your separate ways.

Children who have experienced the break up of their parents' relationship are vulnerable and those who have experienced repeated disappointment, humiliation and inconsistency are the most vulnerable. This is something to consider if you are on the verge of giving up. Children become resilient when they have one or two key people on whom they can rely despite the difficulties of their lives. Loving children is not a prerequisite for acting in their best interests, sometimes you need to do what is right despite your feelings. In this way you become a reliable adult for them, and the chances of building a good relationship with time becomes probable.

Complex and contrasting feelings are natural in the process of forming a stepfamily, there is nothing wrong with adults or children who are struggling with these. Things can be even harder if you think they shouldn't be that way, and have unrealistic expectations of yourself, your family or your ex-partner. We therefore urge you not to expect too much, and to understand that time is a very important factor in the easing of difficult relationships. If you set your sights too high you are likely to be disappointed and feel as if you are failing.

There is professional support available for stepfamilies. A list of these is included at the back of this booklet. Although not always the answer, if you feel stuck or that communication seems to be breaking down seeking help from a counsellor or therapist can sometimes be an extremely useful form of support. Sometimes it feels as if asking for help is a sign of failure, that you should be able to do it for yourself, whereas the reality is that the ability to admit that you need support or help is a strength and one that will help you in building your stepfamily.

In life generally it seems to be easier to pay attention to, and feel bad about what is not working, than to acknowledge and feel good about things that are. Even though sometimes it may feel that you do not have time to look at both sides of the coin, you and your family deserve to recognise your achievements. It is worthwhile to think about what you and your family are doing right, as this will help you all to feel good about yourselves. A stepfamily is a re-investment in family life, if you haven't given up working at it, if you still feel that it is worth persevering, then you are doing well, in fact very well!

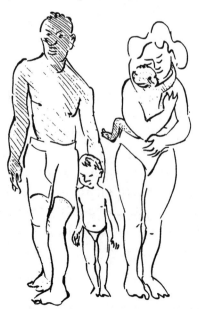

OTHER MATERIALS

All

1. Judy Blume, 1987. LETTERS TO JUDY. Pan Books Ltd. *What Kids Wish They Could Tell You.*

2. A CELEBRATION OF CUSTOMS AND RITUALS OF THE WORLD. Dragon's World Ltd. 1994.

Adults

1. The National Stepfamily Association annotated Book List for Parents and Stepparents.

2. Adele Faber and Elaine Mazlish, 1988. SIBLINGS WITHOUT RIVALRY. Avon Child Care.

3. Adele Faber and Elaine Mazlish, 1982. HOW TO TALK SO KIDS WILL LISTEN AND LISTEN SO KIDS WILL TALK. Avon Child Care.

4. Toby Alexander, 1995. HIS, HERS, THEIRS: A FINANCIAL HANDBOOK FOR STEPFAMILIES. Stepfamily Publications.

5. Wilson, Leslie, 1996. DIARY OF A STEPFATHER. Stepfamily Publications. *A moving account of one man's journey from family to stepfamily.*

6. Kahn, Tim, 1995. LEARNING TO STEP TOGETHER. Stepfamily Publications. *A handbook for parents and stepparents.*

7. Cox, Kathleen, 1995. ANOTHER STEP: WEDDINGS IN STEPFAMILIES. Stepfamily Publications. *Highlighting the complexity and rewards of stepfamily weddings.*

8. Clout, Imogen, 1993. WHERE THERE'S A WILL THERE'S A WAY: MAKING A WILL IN A STEPFAMILY. *A clear guide to the issues and procedures involved.*

9.   De'Ath, Erica, 1993. A NEW BABY IN A STEPFAMILY.
      Stepfamily Publications. *Raising the complex issues for
      and against having a baby in a stepfamily.*

Children and Young People

1.   The National Stepfamily Association annotated Book List
      for Children and Young People.
2.   Clare Harding, 1994. STEPPING OUT: CAN BROOK
      SURVIVE HER OWN STEPFAMILY? Pan Macmillan.
      *Clearly identifiable issues written from the position of
      teenagers whose parents are separating and repartnering.*
3.   Brown, Laurene Krasny and Marc, 1993. DINOSAURS
      DIVORCE. *A clear and supportive guide for young
      children whose parents are divorcing.*
4.   Judy Blume, 1988. IT'S NOT THE END OF THE
      WORLD. Pan Books Ltd. *A 12 year old journey
      through her parents worsening relationship to acceptance
      that her parents will remain apart.*
5.   Danziger, Paula, 1986. THE DIVORCE EXPRESS.
      Heinemann.
      *14 year old Phoebe is having to deal with a split family
      life since her parents' divorce.*
6.   Danziger, Paula, 1991. ITS AN AARDVARK-EAT-
      TURTLE-WORLD. Heinemann.
      Sequel to Divorce Express where stepfamily life is encountered.

Video

1.   The Lowdown: Our New Family. BBC TV.

REFERRAL LIST

1. **The National Stepfamily Association**
   Office Telephone: 0171 209 2460
   STEPFAMILY Telephone Counselling Service: 0990 168 388
   (2.00 - 5.00 pm, 7.00 - 10.00 pm Mon - Fri)

2. **Advice, Advocacy & Representation Service for Children**
   Office Telephone: 0161 839 8442
   Helpline: 0800 616 101 (4.00 - 10.00 pm Mon - Sun)

3. **ChildLine**
   Office Telephone: 0171 239 1000
   Helpline: 0800 1111 (24 hours)
   Children in care: 0800 884 444
   Childline Minicom: 0800 400 222

4. **The Children's Legal Centre Ltd**
   Helpline: 0120 687 3820 (2.00 - 5.00 pm Mon - Fri)
   (10.00 am - 12.00 pm Wed)

5. **Cruse (Bereavement Care)**
   Office Telephone: 0181 940 4818
   Helpline: 0181 332 7227 (Mon-Fri 9.30 am - 5.00 pm)

6. **Kidscape**
   Helpline: 0171 730 3300 (10.00 am - 4.00 pm Tues and Wed)

7. **Meet a Mum Association (MAMA)**
   Helpline: 0181 665 0357 (office hours only)

8. **NSPCC**
   Office Telephone: 0171 825 2500
   Helpline: 0800 800 500 (24 hours)

9. **Asian Family Counselling Service**
   Office Telephone: 0181 997 5749

10. **Home Start UK**
    Office Telephone: 0116 233 9955

11. **Parents at Work**
    Office Telephone: 0171 628 3565·
    Information line: 0171 628 3578

12. **Parentline**
    Office Telephone: 01702 554 782
    Helpline: 01702 559 900 (9.00 - 6.00 Mon - Fri)

13. **Parent Network**
    Office Telephone: 0171 735 4596
    Parent Information Line: 0171 735 1214

14. **Relate (National Marriage Guidance)**
    Office Telephone: 01788 573 241

15. **Citizen Advice Bureaux**
    See entry under Citizen Advice Bureaux in your local
    phone book.

16. **Mind**
    Office telephone: 0181 519 2122
    Legal Advice Line: 0181 519 2122 (2.00 - 4.30 pm,
    Mon, Wed, Fri)
    Information line: 0181 522 1728 (10.00 am - 12.30 pm
    and 2.00 - 4.30 pm Mon - Fri)

17. **Young Minds**
    Office Telephone: 0171 336 8445
    Helpline: 0345 626 376 (9.30 am - 5.30 pm Mon - Fri)
    (24 hour answerphone)

18. **Youth Access**
    Office Telephone: 0181 772 9900